10-
NF-9602
antiques

Smithsonian Institution, National Museum of History and Technology,
photograph by Alfred Tamarin

DOLLS DOLLS DOLLS

Museum of the City of New York, Toy Collection

DOLLS DOLLS D

Shirley Glubok

Special Photography by Alfred Tamarin
Designed by Gerard Nook

FOLLETT PUBLISHING COMPANY
CHICAGO

THE AUTHOR GRATEFULLY ACKNOWLEDGES THE ASSISTANCE OF:

LUCY BISHOP, Peabody Museum, Salem, Massachusetts
E. BOYD, Museum of International Folk Art, Santa Fe, New Mexico
LUCY HO and NOBUKO KAJITANI, The Metropolitan Museum of Art
STUART LUDLUM, Margaret Woodbury Strong Museum, Rochester, New York
CHARLOTTE LA RUE, Museum of the City of New York
MARTIN LIEFER, New York Historical Society
MARY FRANKLIN, Chester County Historical Association
RODRIS ROTH, Smithsonian Institution
JOE BEN WHEAT, University of Colorado Museum
SUSAN VOGEL, Museum of Primitive Art, New York
CAROL ROSENBAUM and HILARY CAWS

And especially the helpful cooperation of:
ELIZABETH ANNE COLEMAN, Brooklyn Museum

PHOTOGRAPHS

Front cover: Chester County Historical Society, West Chester, Pennsylvania,
photograph by Alfred Tamarin
Back cover: University of Colorado Museum,
photograph by Alfred Tamarin
Endpapers: Essex Institute, Salem, Massachusetts

FOR KAREN AND CHERYL NOOK

Text copyright © 1975 by Shirley Glubok. Illustrations copyright © 1975 by Follett Publishing Company,
a division of Follett Corporation. All rights reserved.
No portion of this book may be reproduced in any form without written permission from the publisher.
Manufactured in the United States of America.

ISBN 0-695-40483-0 Titan binding
ISBN 0-695-80483-9 Trade binding

Library of Congress Catalog Card Number: 73-93559

First Printing

Margaret Woodbury Strong Museum, Rochester, New York, photograph by Alfred Tamarin

Since ancient times people everywhere have loved dolls. For countless children all over the world, playthings in the form of people have been little friends. Dolls are loved by so many of us because they can share our happy times and be companions when we feel lonely and comforts when we are sad. Dolls can be magic and carry us into a world of make-believe.

Dolls may be as tiny as a fingernail or larger than a real baby. They are made of many different materials—paper, cloth, tin, wood, leather, clay, corncobs, and plastic, to name just a few. The majority were made as children's playthings, but some were meant for educational purposes or to amuse grown-ups. Most dolls are quiet companions. Others can cry, talk, sing a song, or recite a nursery rhyme, walk, throw kisses, or even drink from a baby bottle.

The Metropolitan Museum of Art, Rogers Fund 1931

Around four thousand years ago this painted wooden figure was buried in an Egyptian tomb in the valley of the Nile River. Ancient Egyptian noblemen often had many wives. Little figures representing their wives were buried beside them in their tombs, in the belief that the women could then be with them forever.

The figures are called paddle dolls because they are in the form of a flat paddle with simple arms and head. The thousands of tiny beads in the great strings of hair were made from black mud. Some women in Egypt still wear the same hairdo as this ancient doll.

The terra-cotta, or baked clay, doll at right was made in Greece around twenty-five hundred years ago. The body and head were molded in one piece; the legs and arms were made separately and then attached with string and pegs, so they could move. Some of the early Greek clay dolls had clothes that could be put on and taken off; the dress on this one is painted.

Girls in ancient Greece dedicated their dolls to the goddess Artemis before getting married.

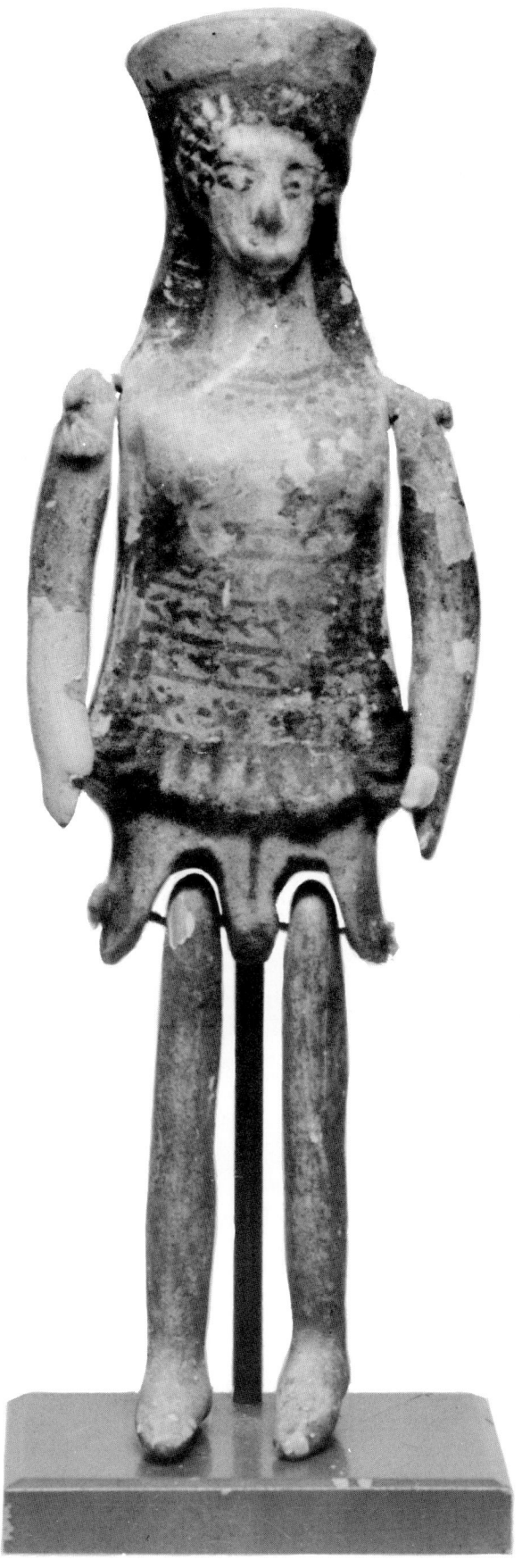

The Metropolitan Museum of Art, Rogers Fund 1944

The Metropolitan Museum of Art, gift of Mrs. Screven Lorillard 1953

Except for ancient figures found in tombs, very few dolls have survived the centuries.

The wooden doll at left was made more than two hundred years ago. She has beautiful features with large eyes painted on her smooth face.

The doll at right was carved of wood in the Alps Mountains more than one hundred and fifty years ago. She is almost three feet tall. Her arms and legs have ball, or round, joints that make them moveable. Her body is also jointed at the waist. One arm is now straight and stiff because the original was lost. Her hairdo and feet were carved and painted.

These dolls, like most made at that time, were modeled by craftsmen who worked in their homes and passed their skills from father to son. To make the doll's head and body, a block of wood was roughly shaped on a machine called a lathe. Hand tools were used to finish the carving. Then the arms and legs were added.

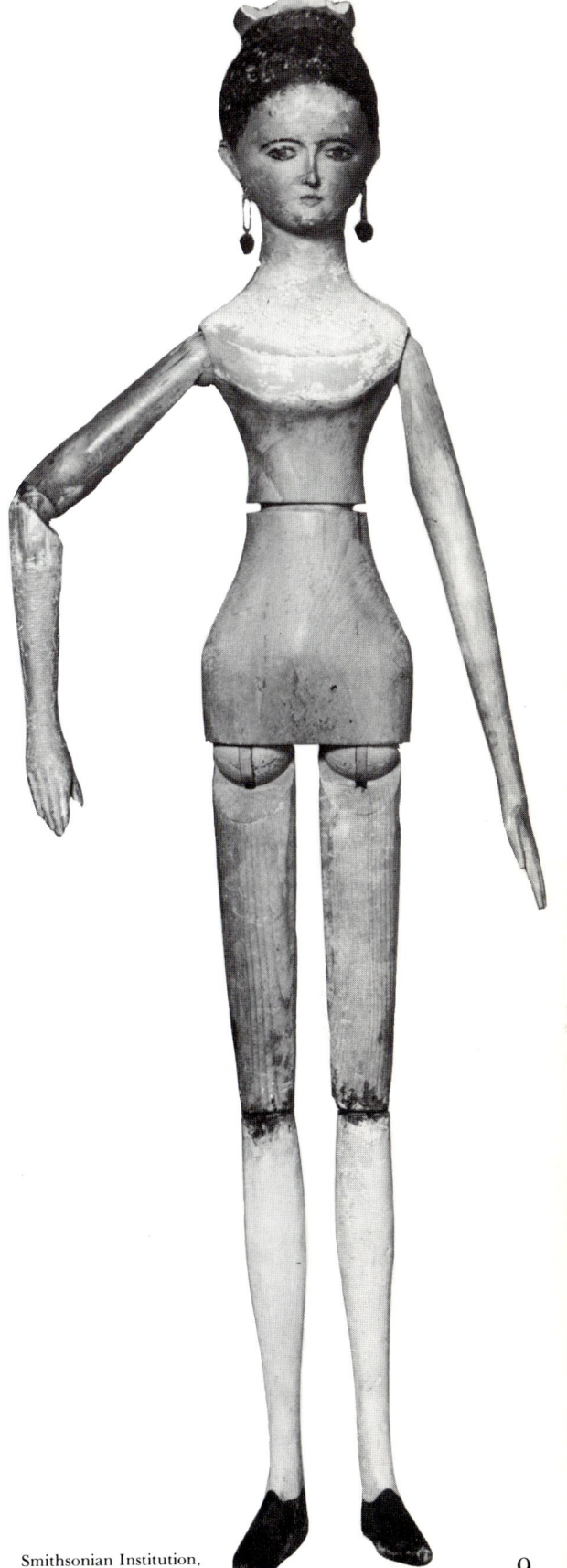

Smithsonian Institution,
National Museum of History and Technology

Margaret Woodbury Strong Museum, photograph by Alfred Tamarin

Wooden dolls were made in all sizes, some as large as life, others less than an inch tall. Many have moveable arms and legs which are sometimes attached to the body by pegs. They are therefore often called peg woodens. Other names for these figures are Dutch dolls because many came from Deutschland, or Germany, and penny woodens because they sometimes were sold for a penny. In later times these dolls were produced in ever greater numbers, and their heads were made of papier-mâché, china, and other materials.

The two dressed dolls at left are from Europe. The third, undressed, was made about one hundred years ago in Vermont from the hard green wood of a rock maple tree. She is sturdy, strong, and durable with sliding joints that let her arms and legs move in different directions. Her hands and feet are made of metal.

Wooden dolls were often dressed in full padded skirts and used as pincushions. Making costumes for dolls was a popular pastime for young ladies who found patterns and suggestions in the ladies' magazines and workbooks of the day.

New York Historical Society

Sometimes dolls were dressed to represent people who walked the streets of England selling their wares. The peddler doll at right has dozens of items to sell, including buttons, brushes, baskets, an umbrella, and even a tiny wooden doll.

A folk ballad tells about a girl named Charlotte who went to a party in an open carriage on a cold, snowy night. Paying no attention to her mother's advice, she refused to wear a coat because she wanted to show off her new dress. She froze to death. The name Frozen Charlotte was given to stiff dolls made of china, with tight fists and bent elbows. Frozen Charlottes are sometimes larger than a foot and a half high. Tiny ones, an inch tall, were often used as favors inside cakes.

Smithsonian Institution,
National Museum of History and Technology

14 Margaret Woodbury Strong Museum,
photograph by Alfred Tamarin

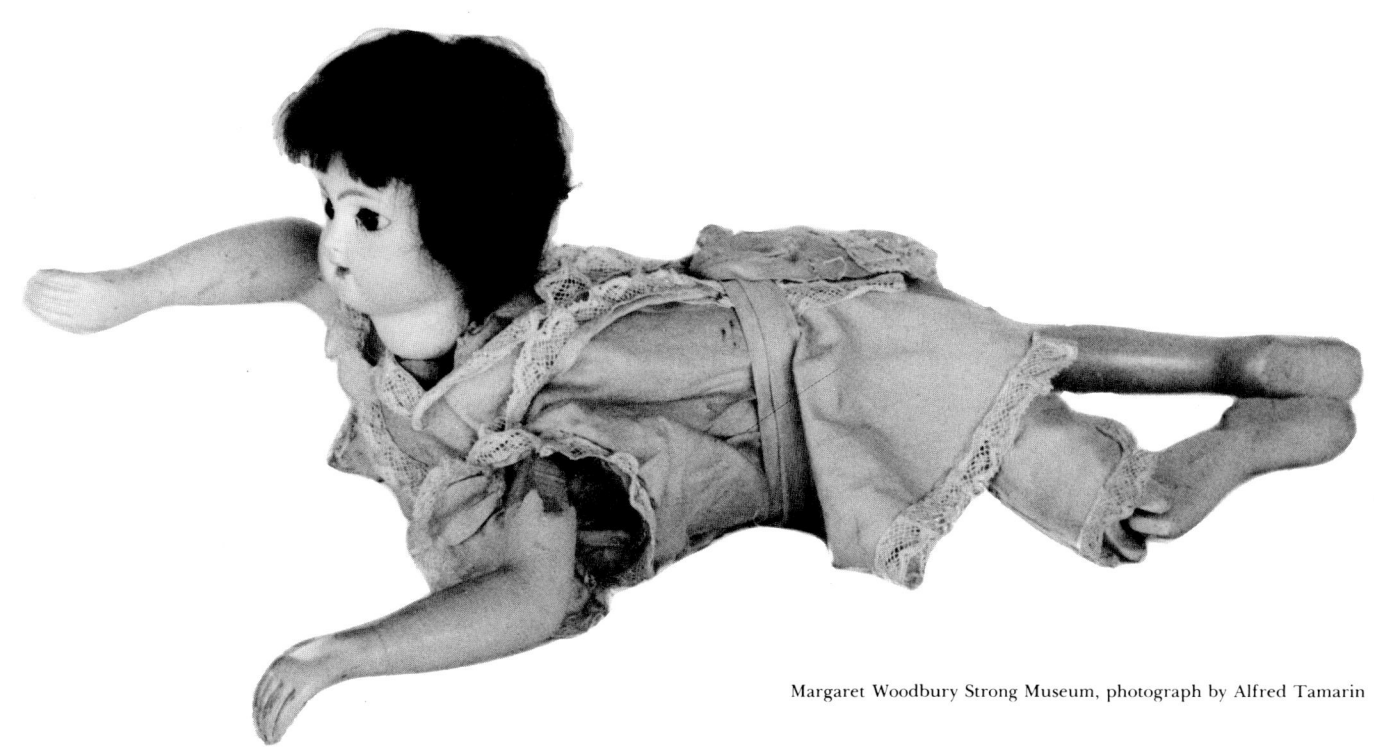

Margaret Woodbury Strong Museum, photograph by Alfred Tamarin

The stiff china-headed lady at left is a mechanical doll called an Autoperipatetikos, a Greek word meaning "self-walking." A turn key winds up the doll's clockwork mechanism which is protected by a cardboard dome hidden under the full skirt. When wound up and set on the floor, the doll waddles along stiffly, moving only her feet. She has leather arms, and she is wearing a dress typical of the American Civil War period. The Autoperipatetikos was invented around 1860.

A mechanical swimming doll, invented in France, was exhibited at the World's Fair in 1879. Her head is bisque, a kind of china that is not shiny, and her body is cork, so she floats on water. Wearing a bathing suit that was the fashion of her day, she can paddle along, moving her arms and legs.

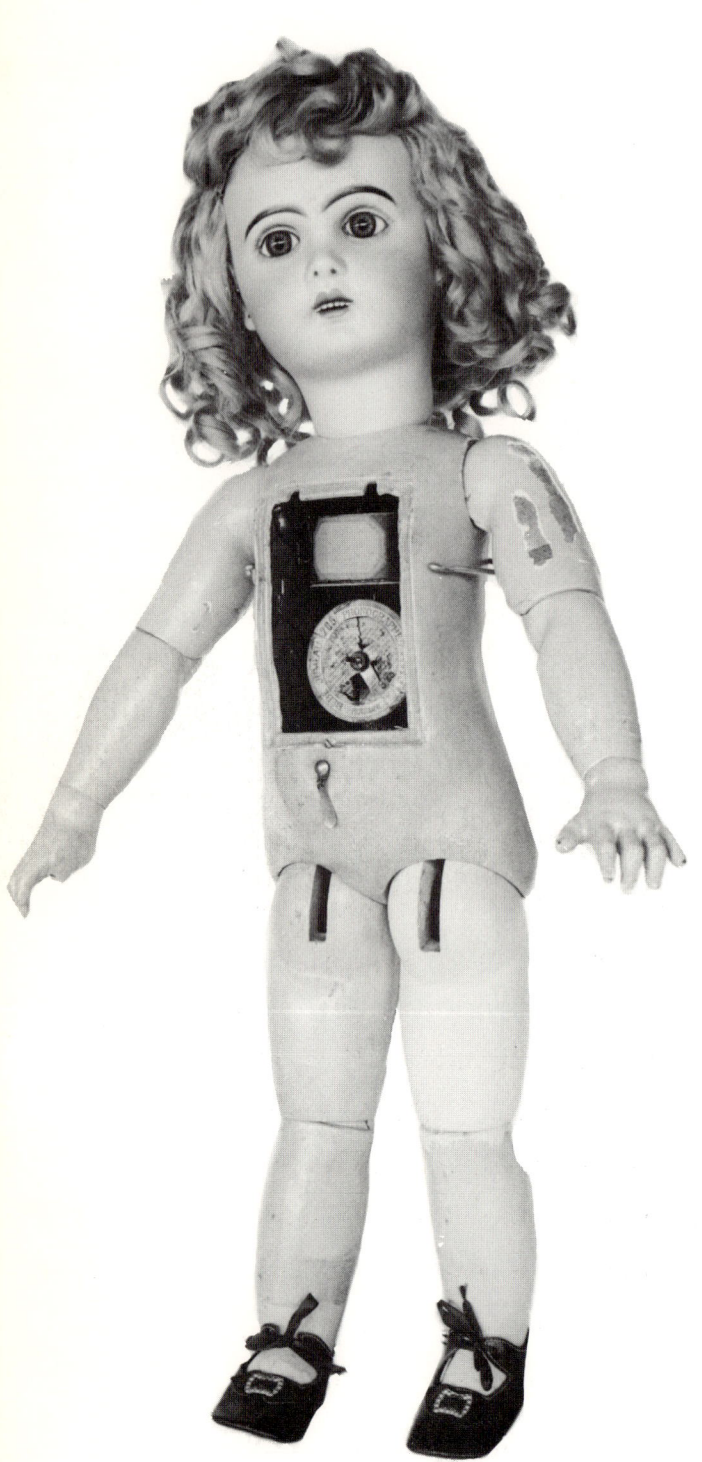

Margaret Woodbury Strong Museum, photograph by Alfred Tamarin

Thomas Edison, inventor of the electric bulb, also invented the mechanism for a talking doll. A little phonograph with disks fits into the doll's body. By changing the disks, the doll's remarks can be changed. Edison dolls operate when a key is turned, winding a spring that works the phonograph.

A windup mechanism starts a music box in the seated lady at right. While the tune plays, her head bobs and her arms move as if she were knitting.

Margaret Woodbury Strong Museum, photograph by Alfred Tamarin

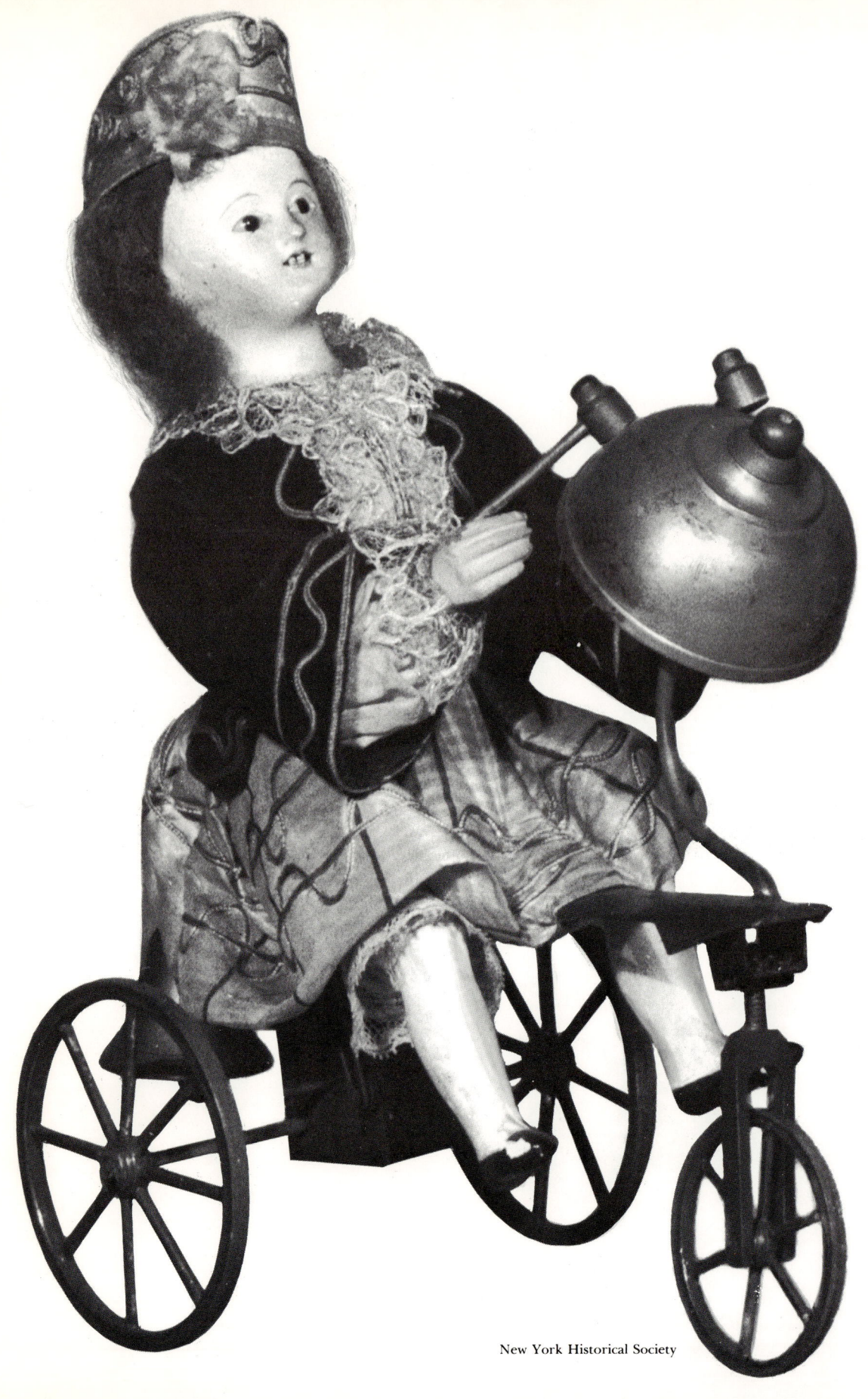

New York Historical Society

Wearing a velvet jacket, taffeta skirt, and fine satin hat, the mechanical doll at left is all dressed up ready to go riding on her tricycle. She is waiting to be wound up so she can tap her little bell as she speeds along on her three wheels.

When pulled by a string, the acrobat team at right can do complicated tricks, turning somersaults and ringing bells. They are dressed as performers, wearing suits decorated with ribbons and lace.

Margaret Woodbury Strong Museum, photograph by Alfred Tamarin

20

New York Historical Society

Margaret Woodbury Strong Museum, photograph by Alfred Tamarin

Pulling a string, pressing a button, or turning a knob on double-faced babies will make their expressions change. The three babies above have crying and smiling faces. The faces that are not showing are hidden under their hoodlike caps. Some dolls have a third face, with closed eyes, as though they were sleeping.

The twin baby dolls at left lie quietly when their carriage is not moving. When the carriage is pushed, the twins cry and wave their hands and feet. The heads of the dolls are made of composition dipped in wax to give a more lifelike appearance. Composition is a mixture of many materials such as plaster of Paris, sawdust, glue, flour, and starch.

Just as there are changes in fashions for ladies' clothes, so there are changes in fashions for dolls' clothes. Before printed magazines advertised the latest styles for ladies, dolls were used to exhibit the new designs from Paris, France, the fashion center of the world. Dress designers made miniature garments for the dolls and sent them all over Europe and to America to show what was being worn in Paris that year. Dolls also showed the latest ladies' hairdos.

Museum of the City of New York,
Toy Collection

The doll at left is elegantly dressed. The stylish outfit she is wearing includes an umbrella. The lovely lady below has a trunk to store her many dresses and her little pocketbook and boots. Some dolls have hats, furs, jewelry, gloves, eyeglasses, combs, and brushes.

Museum of the City of New York,
Toy Collection

This bisque-headed doll with big, beautiful glass eyes wears a dress from the period when it was stylish for women's skirts to reach the floor. The original dress made for the doll at right was worn out or lost, so she is wearing modern clothes. Her ears are pierced, but her earrings also have been lost. The doll's bisque head fits into a socket so it can turn, and her mouth is open to show two teeth. Her body, made of composition, is jointed. The worn hands and torn shoes show that she was much loved and played with by a child.

Margaret Woodbury Strong Museum, photograph by Alfred Tamarin

The word "doll" did not come into use in America until less than two hundred years ago. Before that time all dolls were called "babies," even though most of them were in the form of grown ladies. Today the English word "baby" or the French word "bébé" is used only to refer to a doll representing an infant or small child.

The four babies on the following pages are wearing children's fashions from the past.

Smithsonian Institution,
National Museum of History and Technology

25

26

Smithsonian Institution,
National Museum of History and Technology

Margaret Woodbury Strong Museum,
photograph by Alfred Tamarin

Margaret Woodbury Strong Museum, photograph by Alfred Tamarin

Margaret Woodbury Strong Museum, photograph by Alfred Tamarin

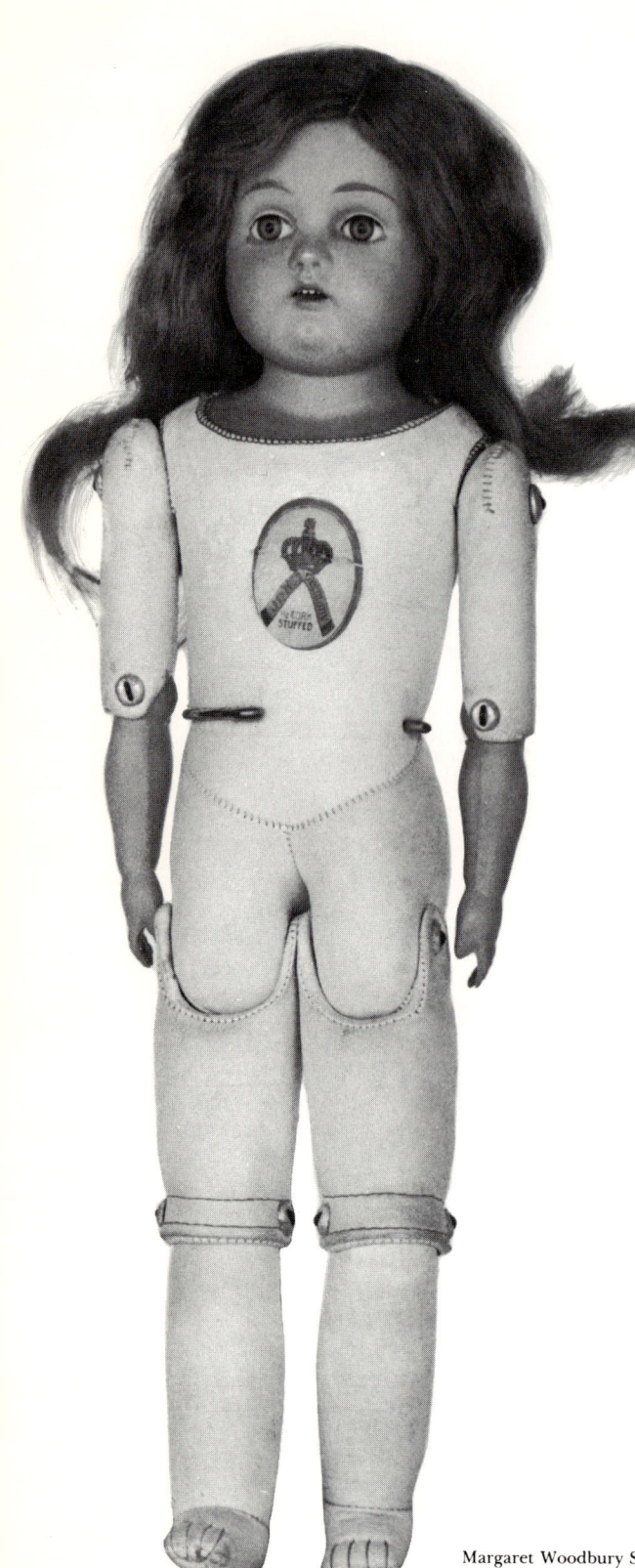

Margaret Woodbury Strong Museum, photograph by Alfred Tamarin

Dolls can be made to look almost any age by changing their clothes, but often those representing very young children have round faces, short necks, and chubby bodies. This undressed doll with real hair and eyes that open and shut has a bisque head, bisque arms, and a leather body stuffed with cork. Her arms and legs can swing, but they cannot move in all directions, like a fully jointed doll's.

An infant doll called Bye-Lo Baby took the part of a real baby in a motion picture called "New Toys" in 1925. The doll's head, which is

Margaret Woodbury Strong Museum, photograph by Alfred Tamari

life-size, was modeled after a three-day-old baby. The woman who designed it looked at hundreds of newborn infants in hospitals until she found the perfect one for her model. She copied its every feature—narrowed eyes, closed mouth, and fat folds at the neck. The doll cries like a three-day-old and wears real baby diapers, dress, cap, and booties. Bye-Lo Baby is one of the most popular dolls ever made.

Museum of the City of New York, Toy Collection

Margaret Woodbury Strong Museum, photograph by Alfred Tamarin

An infant doll in a long dress was a gift to a little girl from her father on her first birthday. On each birthday thereafter, he gave her a new doll, a bigger one each year, until she was nine years old. The smallest is only five inches tall; the largest is nearly two feet. All have bisque heads and were made in Germany.

Above, nine little china dolls are snuggled up in a slipper with their mother. She represents the nursery rhyme character—the old woman who lived in a shoe and had so many children she did not know what to do.

Peabody Museum, Salem, Massachusetts, photograph by M. W. Sexton

Through the ages rag dolls have been popular because the materials are easily available and the dolls are simple to design and sew. The cuddly baby at left was made of soft animal skin by an Alaskan Eskimo. She wears a parka trimmed with fur and soft skin boots called mukluks. Her hair, made of wool yarn, is tied into braids and decorated with beads.

Perhaps the most popular cloth doll of all time is the main character in a series of books by Johnny Gruelle—Raggedy Ann. She has round black eyes and a smiling mouth. Raggedy Anns are loved by children because they are soft, cuddly, and unbreakable.

Museum of the City of New York, Toy Collection

According to old Scotch legends, brownies were fairy creatures who lived in forests. Palmer Cox thought brownies brought good luck, and he wrote stories for children about their adventures. Brownie dolls are good-natured figures with smiling faces, fat bodies, and thin legs. Cloth printed with brownie patterns could be bought and the dolls cut out, sewn up, and stuffed with cotton or sawdust at home.

Margaret Woodbury Strong Museum, photograph by Alfred Tamarin

President Theodore Roosevelt's hunting adventures inspired the name of the stuffed animal who became known the world over as teddy bear. The teddy bear below, with moveable arms and legs, once belonged to children in the Roosevelt family.

Teddy bear was used as a model for Smokey the Bear, the symbol of forest-fire prevention. Many children's stories have been written about teddy bears. Perhaps the best-loved are those by A. A. Milne about Winnie-the-Pooh.

Smithsonian Institution,
National Museum of
History and Technology

Collection of Maurice Sendak, photograph by Alfred Tamarin

A recent book by Maurice Sendak, *Where the Wild Things Are,* inspired the doll at left. In the story a little boy named Max takes an imaginary trip to a place inhabited by strange creatures called "wild things." The doll, made of stuffed cloth, has human hair. Its teeth, claws, and horns are papier-mâché.

Mickey Mouse, created by Walt Disney in the 1930s, is the hero of many comic strips and animated cartoons. Mickey talks and walks like a man. He wears short pants with large buttons and big shoes and gloves. This Mickey Mouse doll is made of stuffed cloth. His felt ears are flat and floppy.

Collection of Maurice Sendak,
photograph by Alfred Tamarin

37

A comic strip character created by Carl Schultze was the subject for a molded felt doll called Foxy Grandpa. He is a humorous figure with a smiling face, fat tummy, and knobby knees. Because of his large shoes, he can stand upright.

Smithsonian Institution,
National Museum of History and Technology,
photograph by Alfred Tamarin

Museum of the City of New York, Toy Collection

Magazine stories and books inspired the Kewpie dolls, imaginary Cupidlike creatures with large eyes and topknots created by Rose O'Neill. The dolls were sold and also given away as prizes at carnivals and amusement parks. As Kewpies grew more popular, they were manufactured in a large variety of materials and sizes, and many imitations were made. The pair above is playing with a toy tea set with Kewpies painted on each piece. Some Kewpies were dressed to represent such people as farmers, firemen, and policemen.

39

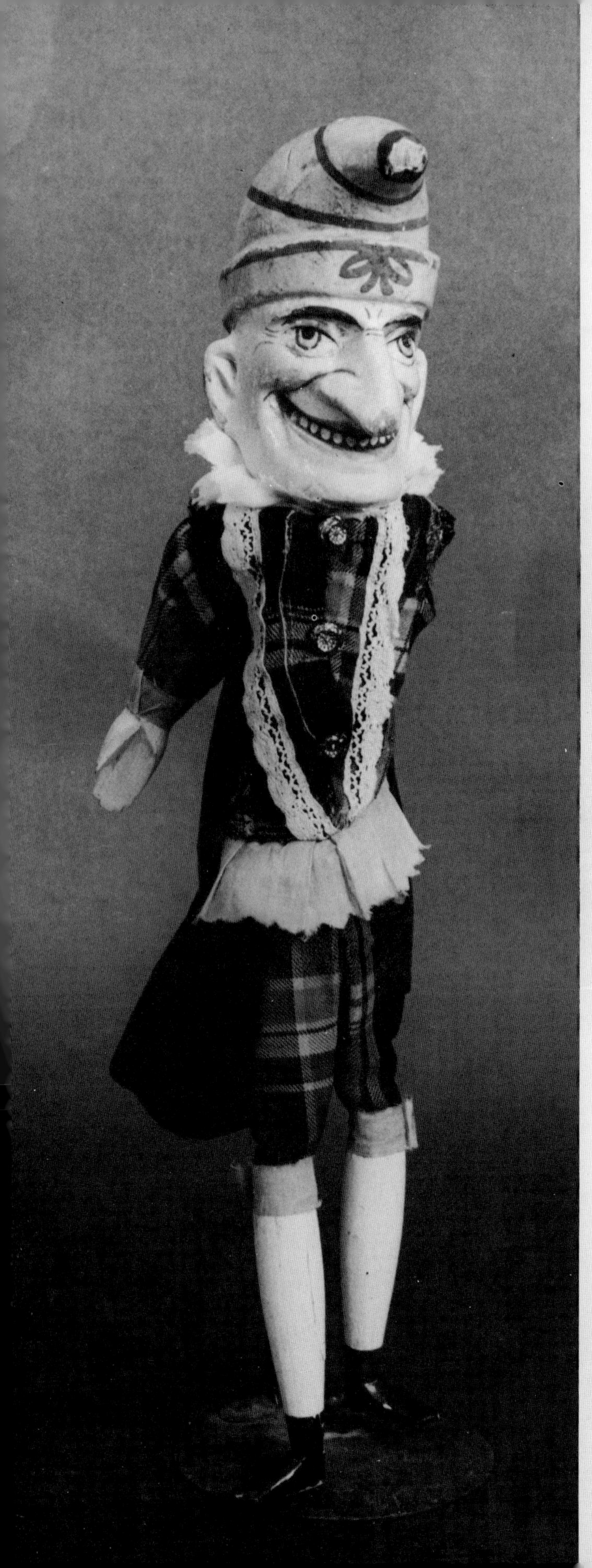

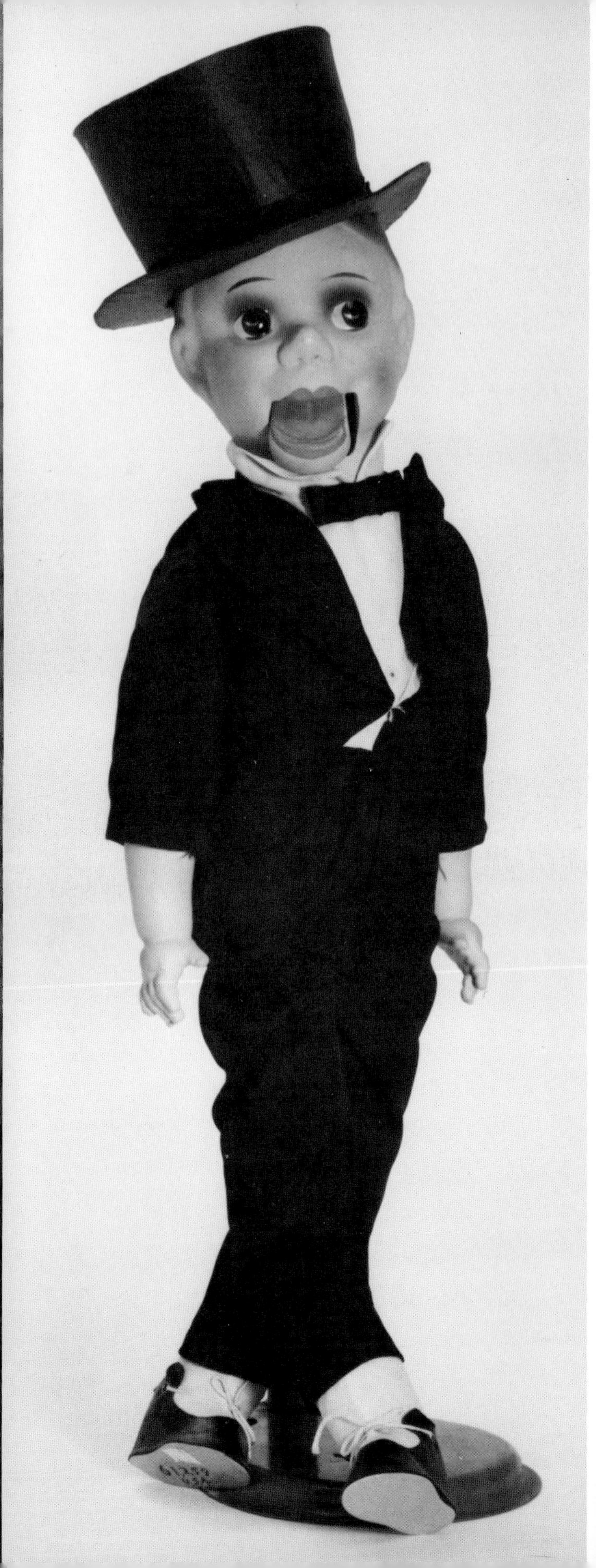

Museum of New Mexico Collection,
photograph by Alfred Tamarin

Smithsonian Institution,
National Museum of
History and Technology

A puppet Polichinelle, as he was originally called, is known by all who have seen a Punch and Judy show. Punch dolls have a long nose and a large chin and wear short trousers and a pointed cap.

Charlie McCarthy dolls, wearing a top hat and a tuxedo, or evening suit, were copied from the dummy that ventriloquist Edgar Bergen used to entertain millions of people over the radio. A ventriloquist can talk without moving his lips and make it seem as if the voice is coming from his dummy.

Shirley Temple dolls were popular in the 1930s when the child movie star was tap dancing and singing in films. This one is made of composition. Dolls that represent well-known personalities are known as character dolls.

Margaret Woodbury Strong Museum,
photograph by Alfred Tamarin

Children can learn nursery rhymes, ABCs, multiplication tables, names of flowers, flags of all nations, and other interesting subjects from illustrated dolls. Their cloth bodies are printed with words, numbers, and pictures. They have china heads and bisque arms and legs.

Paper dolls have always been popular because they are cheap to buy or simple to make on one's own. Printed paper dolls with paper clothes come in books and popular magazines ready to be cut out. Or dolls and their wardrobes are easily homemade with only plain paper and crayons. The ballerina at right can be dressed in various costumes for her performances on the stage.

Margaret Woodbury Strong Museum, photograph by Alfred Tamarin

Museum of the City of New York, Toy Collection

Collection of Frank P. Davidson, Esq., photograph by Alfred Tamarin

Many children like to play war games with toy soldiers which can be organized into armies to fight new battles or to recreate famous battles in history. The group proudly riding their fine horses are hand-painted French lead soldiers.

Grown-ups often collect models of soldiers of different regiments in various armies. The standing lead soldier represents an officer who fought in the Royal Dragoon Guards of the British cavalry. His uniform is complete with a shoulder belt that holds a pouch for cartridges, a saber, and a tall helmet with a feathered crest.

The Soldier Shop, New York, photograph by Alfred Tamarin

The stuffed cloth Polish boy at left wearing wooden shoes is ready to beat his drum with his little mittenlike hands. His cheerful features are painted on his simple round face. An armature, or wire skeleton, inside the cloth body makes the doll stand stiffly in position.

The Italian boy at right shows how lifelike cloth dolls can be. He is made of felt which was molded into shape and stuffed. His features are painted, and his curls are made of mohair. His body is flexible so that his arms and legs can be placed in various positions. The little boy is very well dressed, wearing knickers and knitted socks.

Museum of New Mexico Collection,
photograph by Alfred Tamarin

Margaret Woodbury Strong Museum,
photograph by Alfred Tamarin

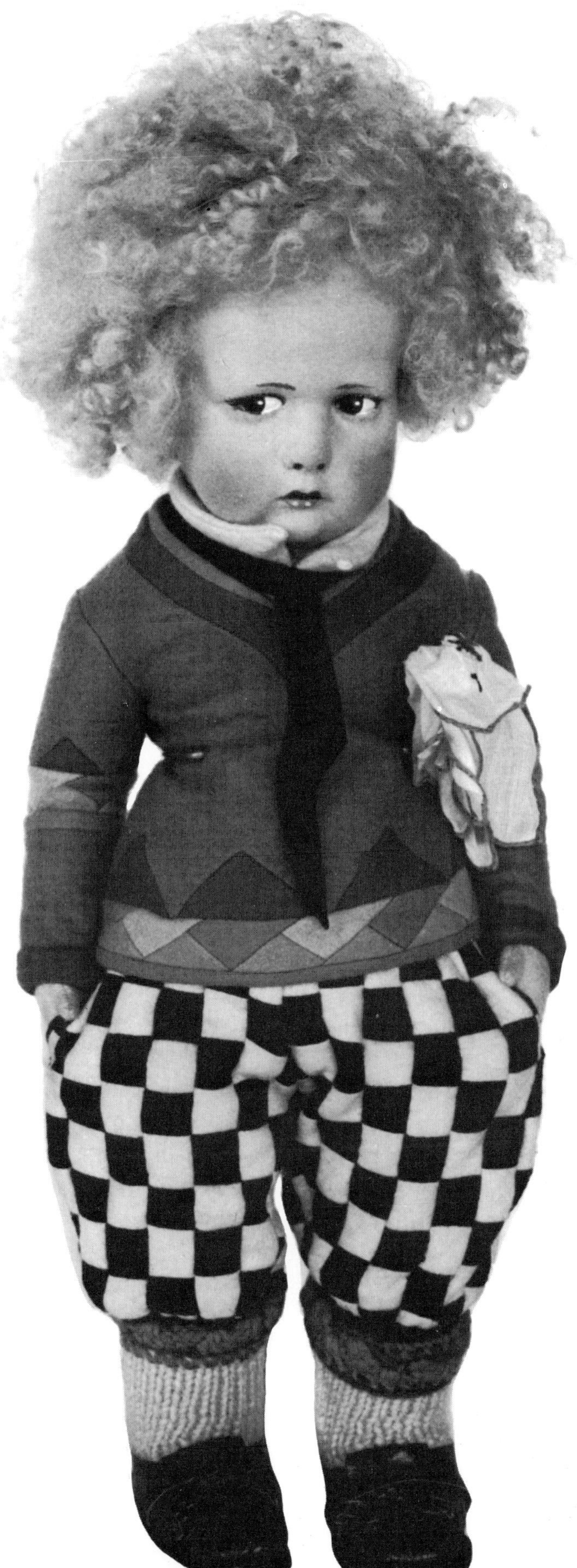

Margaret Woodbury Strong Museum

Through the years grown women as well as little girls have loved dollhouses. The elegant one at left is made of wood. It has a door, windows, chimneys, and even a little balcony and fence. Lace curtains and shades hang at the windows.

For almost one hundred and fifty years a family of dolls has lived in a miniature house in New York City. The little family still has much of the original furniture, and as the years went by, they have acquired more treasures, such as musical instruments, pictures, fine objects of silver, and a library of rare books. A room from the dollhouse is shown below. The entire house, decorated for Christmas, can be seen on the following pages.

Museum of the City of New York, Toy Collection

Museum of the City of New York, Toy Collection

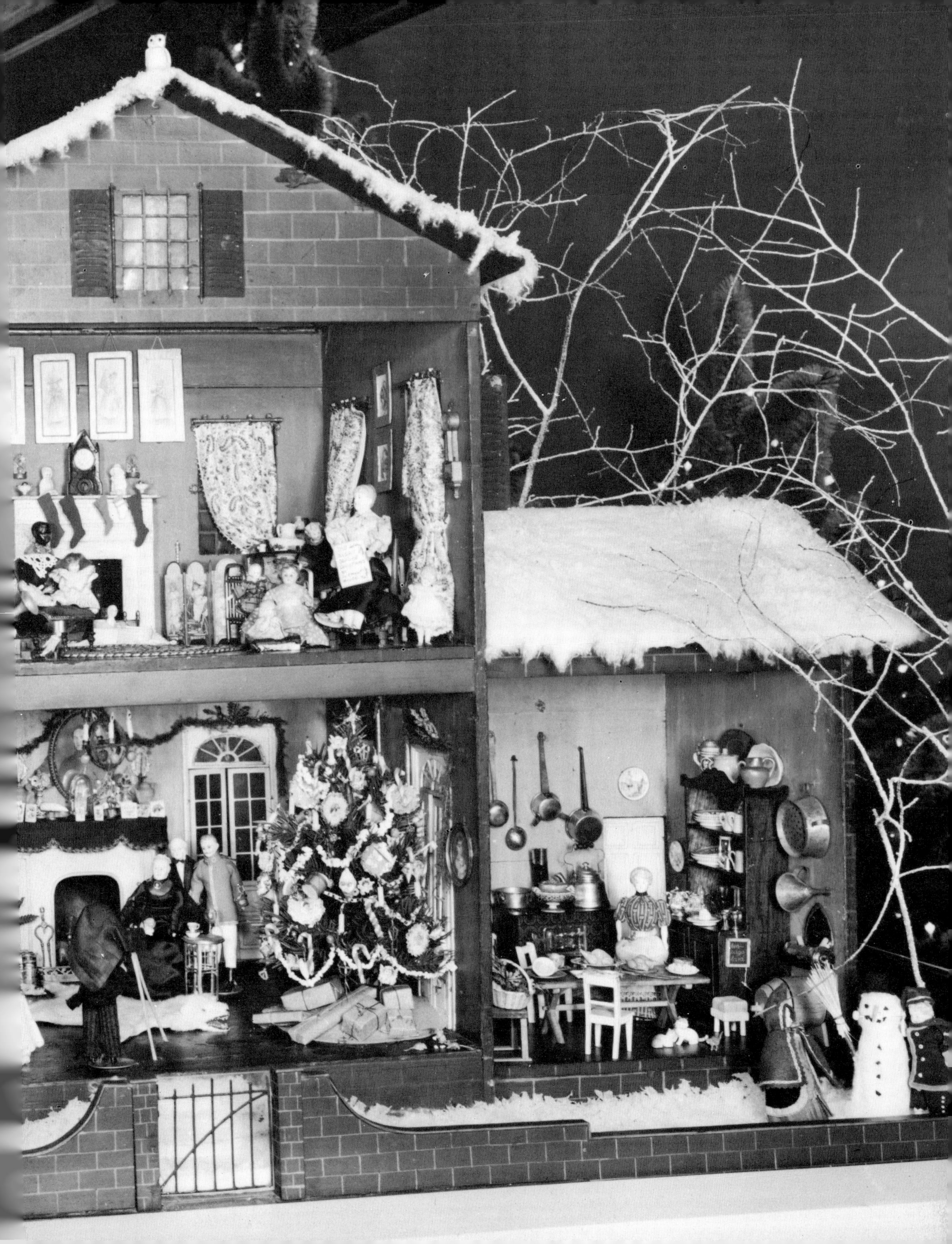

The Metropolitan Museum of Art, The Sylmaris Collection, gift of George C. Graves 1930

This old-fashioned toy kitchen is fully equipped with everything needed for cooking, including tiny utensils hanging over the fireplace. Miniature dishes, pitchers, chopping boards, bowls, and an oil-burning lamp can be identified.

An old wooden doll with glass eyes and an old-fashioned dress stands before a miniature chest of drawers at right. The chest was made for a mayor of New York City in Colonial times. Even the tiny china bowls on top are about two hundred years old.

Museum of the City of New York, Toy Collection

Museum of the City of New York, Toy Collection

An elegant ten-room house, including gardens and bathrooms, was designed by a New York woman around fifty years ago. It is complete in every detail, with floor coverings, furniture, and even plants. The owner of the dollhouse had many artist friends who made miniature statues and paintings for one of the rooms, an art gallery. On the floor above the gallery is a little porch where a tray with a tiny pitcher and glasses and a bowl of fruit are waiting to be served as refreshments to visitors.

Every workaday item imaginable is included in the dollhouse. The laundry room is furnished with a basket full of clothespins and even starch. Tiny towels hang in the bathroom, and miniature medicine bottles sit on a nearby shelf. A bar of Ivory soap on the sink ledge and a piece of plastic in the washbowl make it appear that there is water in the sink.

Museum of the City of New York, Toy Collection

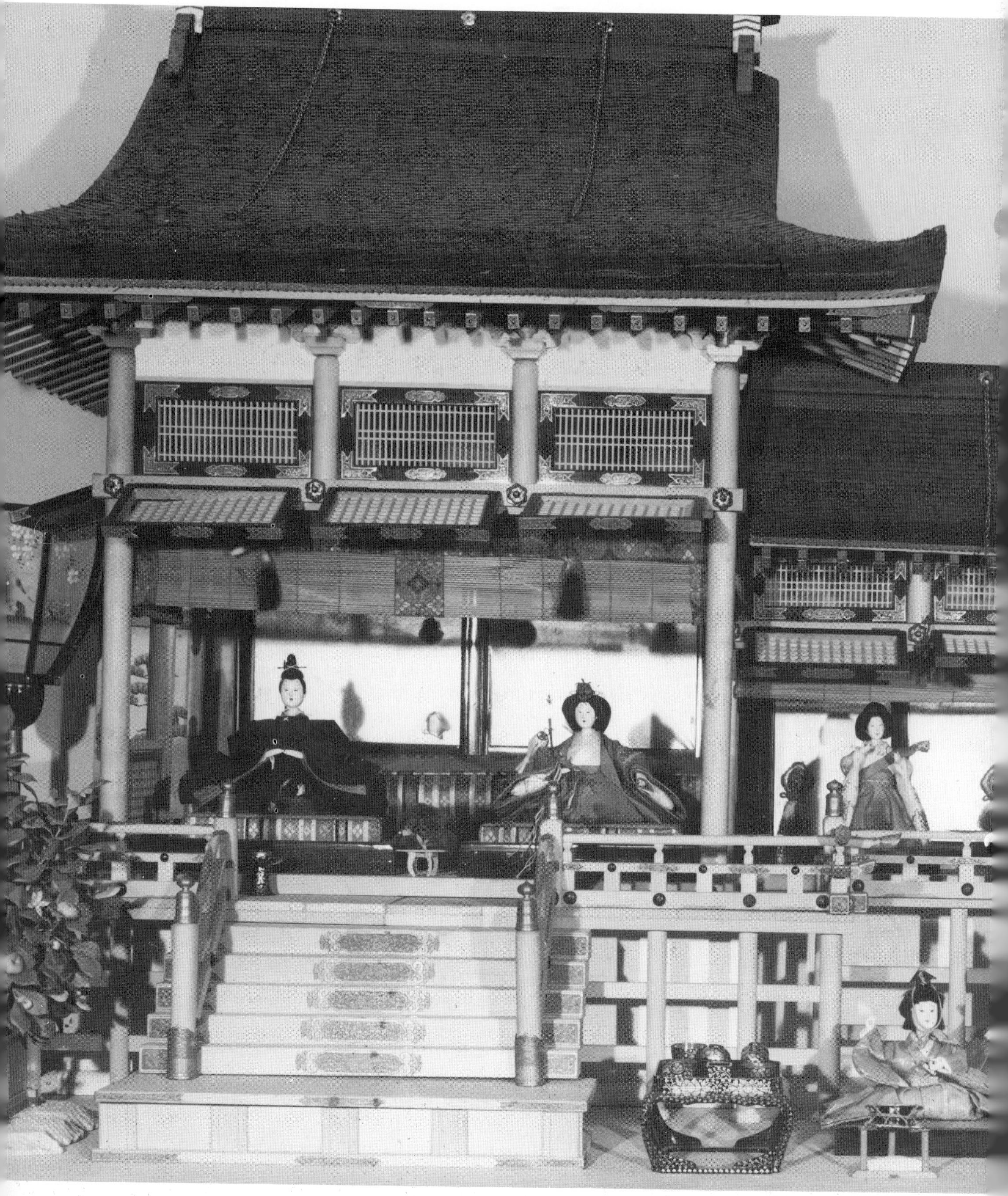

This model of a Japanese emperor's palace is complete with furniture and utensils used by the imperial household. It was displayed in the Girls' Day festival that is celebrated in Japan every year on March 3. In this court scene ceremonial dolls dressed in traditional costumes representing the emperor and the empress are seated on their thrones. They are attended by ladies-in-waiting, while court musicians play for them.

During the Boys' Day festival, held on May 5, dolls representing famous men in history are displayed. Rather than celebrating their birthdays on the day they were born, Japanese children are given presents on the day of the festival.

Peabody Museum, Salem, Massachusetts, photograph by M. W. Sexton

58

University of Colorado Museum,
photograph by Alfred Tamarin

University of Colorado Museum, photograph by Alfred Tamarin

At left is a Chinese bride doll dressed in embroidered silk. Pearls and jewels hang from her headdress which has a cloth veil that would be pulled over her face during the wedding ceremony. Colors are significant to the Chinese. Traditionally, brides wear red, a color that is chosen for happy occasions.

The knitted doll above was made in the South American country of Peru. Since ancient times Peruvians have been highly skilled in knitting, embroidering, and weaving.

The British Museum, London

In Africa Ashanti women and girls carry around flat dolls tucked into wide waistcloths, which are designed to carry babies. The dolls are religious objects. They are used in the hope of having beautiful children. The doll at left fits the Ashanti ideal of beauty, with long neck, round face, tiny mouth, and high forehead. Women and girls play with the dolls, bathing and dressing them.

Pueblo Indian children in the southwestern United States have dolls to teach them about the kachinas, spirits who live in mountains and clouds and at the bottom of springs and lakes. To honor the kachinas, the Pueblo hold ceremonial dances. They wear masks and costumes and paint their bodies, acting as if they had become the spirits. There are many different kachinas, each identified by a different mask. Dolls representing them are given to the children during intermission of the dances.

Kachina dolls are made of pine or the roots of dead cottonwood trees. Their faces are painted to represent the various masks worn by the ceremonial dancers. The Zuni Yamuhakto kachina at right wears a costume of cloth, wool yarn, and feathers.

University of Colorado Museum, photograph by Alfred Tamarin

A Sioux Indian of the Great Plains of South Dakota made the doll at left. She has a cloth head and painted features. Long beads hang from her ears and cover her jacket, and her moccasins and leggings are decorated with tiny round beads of glass. Round metal disks at her waist represent the silver belts made by Plains Indians.

Peabody Museum, Salem, Massachusetts, photograph by M. W. Sexton

University of Colorado Museum, photograph by Alfred Tamarin

This pair of dolls represents a Navajo man and woman. The Navajo are American Indians who live in the Southwest. Both dolls are wearing velvet shirts decorated with fancy buttons, a traditional Navajo fashion. The tribe is famous for making beautiful silver and turquoise jewelry. Necklaces, earrings, and bracelets are worn proudly by men as well as women.

The dolls are made of stuffed cloth. Simple rectangles and squares stitched on with thread indicate the mouths, noses, eyes, and brows.

63

University of Colorado Museum, photograph by Alfred Tamarin

Eskimo people in the Far North wear fur parkas with the fur on the inside for extra warmth. Their tall boots are also furry. The modern Eskimo dolls above are made of stuffed cloth with embroidered stitches for their eyes, nose, and mouth.

Over the years millions of dolls have been made for millions of children who loved and cared for them. The children finally wore the dolls out or broke them, then discarded them. But luckily some old dolls have been preserved for us to admire and study, and new ones are constantly being made for children to play with. The story of these dolls tells us much about the story of mankind.